internet @ction

Chilling Out

Anne Rooney

Illustrated by Debi Ani

Big Fish

First published in the UK in 2000 by
Big Fish, an imprint of C&B Children's Books,
London House, Great Eastern Wharf,
Parkgate Road, London SW11 4NQ
www.bigfishonline.co.uk

ISBN 1 903174 19 8

British Library Cataloguing in
Publication Data for this book is
available from the British Library

Printed in Hong Kong

Project management: Honor Head
Editor: Anna Claybourne
Designer: Angela Ashton
Illustrator: Debi Ani
Menu bar icons: Chris Swee

Screen shots of Microsoft Internet Explorer
on pages 9 and 43 used by permission of
Microsoft Corporation.

CONTENTS

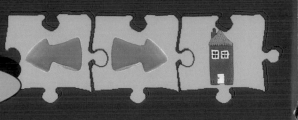

Welcome to **Internet @ction: Chilling Out.** We've put together all the coolest things you can do on the Internet – so if you're ready to take a trip into deepest cyberspace, pack and prepare for blast-off!

What is the Internet?

The Internet, or Net, is a huge, tangled network of links between computers all over the world. It's a bit like the road system, except it's for moving information instead of things and people. It can carry messages, text, pictures, video, animation – in fact, any sort of information that can be put in electronic form. Computers on the Net are linked by cables and phone lines.

What can I use it for?

Lots of people use the Net for work, for writing letters and for finding stuff out. It's also great for helping with your homework. But the Internet is also for having fun – and that's what **Chilling Out** is all about. Whether you want to work or have fun, here are some of the things you can do:

■ **E-mailing** With e-mail you can send electronic messages to people all over the world. It's the quickest, easiest and cheapest way to keep in touch with your friends – wherever they are.

■ **Surfing the Web** The World Wide Web is a huge collection of information – words, pictures, music, video and more – stored on computers all over the world. The information is put on 'pages' which you look at on your screen. Most web pages are linked into groups called websites, and many have links to other sites, so you can go exploring (also called browsing or websurfing) at the click of a button.

■ **Chatting** Instead of chatting on the phone, chat on the Net! It's cheap and it's fun. You type a message, and the person you're chatting with can see it immediately and type you an instant reply.

■ **Taking part** Once you've got the hang of it, make your own website and join the wired community!

If you're stuck with schoolwork, check out **Internet @ction: Homework Busters.** It's a cool book that shows you everything you need to know about using the Net to help with homework.

Venturing out

The next few pages will tell you what you need to go on-line and how to get started. Then you can look forward to exploring the Net! We'll look around the World Wide Web and find things to do and places to go, both in cyberspace and when you're relaxing off-line. You can send e-mail and cards to your friends – even postcards from the places in cyberspace you've visited. You can make new friends to chat to, do some useful work, blob in front of a cartoon, collect freebies, watch the world go by, play on-line games, read an e-zine and even make your own website. So fasten your seatbelt, and we'll be off...

Don't wait for us

If you've used the Web before, you can pick up from any point in the book and take off straight away. But if you're new to the Internet, or haven't had a lot of practice, you'll probably need a bit more help. That's why this book starts with some really simple stuff that'll help you get the hang of the Net. Working through the next few pages will bring you up to speed with basic Web skills. Once you've got the hang of these, you'll be ready to move on and try some more advanced tricks. Then it's fast forward all the way to becoming a whizz on the Web! By the time you reach the end of the book, you'll be chilling out with the coolest of cyber surfers!

You're bound to come across all kinds of new words and jargon to do with the Internet. If you're feeling overloaded with technobabble, check out the glossary on page 46.

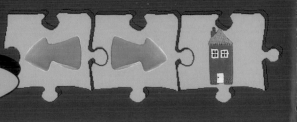

If your computer's never been into cyberspace before, you'll need to do a little tuning up to get it ready. Ask for some help if you need it.

What do you need to get started?

You'll need:

- **A computer** It doesn't have to be the flashiest model in the shops, as long as it's not too ancient. You can't use a games console – but you might be able to use your cable TV and set-top box as a computer.

- **A modem** This is a bit of equipment that changes signals from your computer so that they can travel down the phone lines. You need to plug the modem into the computer and into a phone socket – so you need a phone socket as well! Some modems look like small boxes, while others come as 'cards' which fit inside your computer. Your computer might have a modem fitted already. If not, find out as much as you can about your computer before you go to the shops – you want to make sure you buy the right modem.

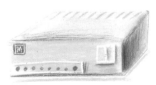

- **An Internet Service Provider, or ISP** This is a company that helps your computer link up to the Internet. When you go on-line, your computer uses the modem to check into the ISP's computer. That's your gateway to the Internet – then the World Wide Web's your oyster! Some ISPs charge for their services – but lots are free. Your ISP will give you a CD-ROM with the software you need to get on-line and connect to their computer. You can often get CDs for free ISPs in shops or on the covers of magazines. (If you don't have a CD-ROM drive, you can phone and ask them to send you floppy disks. Remember to tell them whether you've got a Mac or PC.)

- **A web browser** This is the software that helps you find your way around the Web. There will be a browser on the CD you get from your ISP, and your computer may have one anyway. The most common web browsers are Microsoft® Internet Explorer and Netscape® Navigator (or Communicator) – you've probably got one of these. There's more about browsers on pages 8 and 44.

Telephone time

Remember that when you're on-line, you'll probably be charged the price of a local phone call. Calls to your ISPs may be free, but if not, before you go on the Net make sure you ask the person who pays the bill. People can also get annoyed if you're on-line when they want to use the telephone! So it's a good idea to agree with everyone else in your family about who can use the Net, when, and for how long.

You're special

We're all different, and some people are better at some things than others. If you can't see very well, or maybe have difficulty hearing or controlling your fingers, there are things you can do to make using the computer easier. If you find it hard, get someone to help you change the settings, or even fit some extra bits and pieces to help you. Your computer will let you change things like the size and colours of the display on the screen, and the size and speed of the mouse pointer. You can also get special dictation software that lets you talk to the computer instead of using a mouse and a keyboard. And you can get special hardware – like a touchscreen, or a trackerball instead of a mouse. If you think you might need any of these things, get someone to help you set them up so that you can work better on your own from now on.

Get your mum or dad, or another grown–up, to look at the Grown–up zone page at the end of this book. This will show them how to give you your own personal space on the computer.

Making your pointer bigger makes it much easier to see!

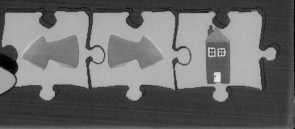

Go!

So, you're ready to start! We'll begin with the Web, because it's the part of the Internet everyone wants to know about. On this page you can find out the basics – and get surfing!

Get going

When you're ready to go, make sure your modem is plugged in.

■ If your computer hasn't been connected to the Internet before, put the CD-ROM from your ISP in the drive and follow the instructions. It will take you through the steps you need to connect to their computer and set up your account. You'll need to give some details about yourself and choose a name to use on-line.

There's more about choosing a name and a password on page 22.

The CD-ROM will also check that you've got a web browser, or set one up for you if you haven't. When you've finished setting up, you're ready to surf!

■ If your computer's an old hand at web browsing, just launch your web browser. You can do this by double-clicking its icon on the desktop, or choosing it from a menu.

You're on the Web!

The first web page you will see is called your 'home page'. It's the one that always opens when you go on-line. The home page that comes up will have been chosen by your ISP, or the manufacturer of your computer, or someone else who has used your computer. It may be a useful starting point, such as a search engine – a page that will help you to find what you want – or it may just be a load of advertising that you really don't want to see every day. Later, you'll find out how to choose your own home page so that you start from somewhere useful or fun. For now, let's just look at the browser window.

Quicklinks
The address of the **Internet @ction** website is: **http://www. internetaction.co.uk**. A web address like this is called a URL. Find out more about them on page 10.

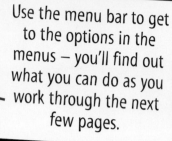

This line shows the address of the web page you're looking at. You can type another address in here to go to a different page.

Use the menu bar to get to the options in the menus – you'll find out what you can do as you work through the next few pages.

Welcome to my Web Page - Microsoft Internet Explorer [Working Offline]

File   Edit   View   Favorites   Tools   Help

Back   Forward   Stop   Refresh   Home   Search   Favorites   History   Mail

Address

Go

The web page you're at will appear in this space.

Use the toolbar for things you want to do a lot, like move backwards and forwards. You'll find out what you can do with this very soon.

Done   My Computer

On the next few pages, you'll find out how to use the browser window to find  the website or web page you want, and how to move around in cyberspace quickly and easily.

What are those boxes?

Throughout the book, you'll find green 'Quicklinks' boxes like the one below, with a little picture in the corner (called an icon). Whenever you see a Quicklinks box, it means we've lined up some cool websites for you to look at. You can link to them straight away through the **Internet @ction** website.

Once you've got started on the Web, you can cruise around as you please.

You can go surfing alone, or with a friend or a brother or sister.

Quicklinks
All you have to do is ask your browser to go to the **Internet @action** website. From there, you'll be able to follow easy links to the other websites we've suggested.

When you explore any new place, it's a good idea to start close to home and not wander too far away until you've got your bearings. These two pages show you how to start on the Web by going to a few friendly websites.

Got the address?

There are web pages on every topic you can imagine – and lots you can't. That means there are a lot of web pages. The most recent estimates are that there are over a billion. Luckily, each web page has its own address. It's called a URL (pronounced Yoo-Ar-El), which is short for Unique Resource Locator. Here's a typical URL, broken down into its main parts so you can see how it works.

> When you type a URL, it doesn't matter whether you use small letters or capitals.

> This is the part of the server where the page is stored.

http://www.internetaction.co.uk/co/index.html

> This part shows that this is a web page. Almost all Net addresses begin with this.

> This part of the address shows you who the site belongs to.

> This is the filename of the home page – the first page of the website.

Then type it in!

After you've started up your browser, you'll see a box, usually near the top. This is where you type in the URL of the website you want to go to.

Go to:

You don't need to type the 'http://' bit, as the browser provides this.

Following the links

Once you've got to a page you want, you might find there are links to other pages that look interesting. A link can be:

A word that is shown in a different colour, or underlined

click here

A button or icon

A picture

When you move the mouse pointer over a link, it changes to a pointing hand, like this. Click on the link to follow it and go to the next web page.

Find more addresses

There are loads of places where you can find the addresses of cool websites. Newspapers and magazines list the URLs of the best sites they've found, and you often see URLs on advertisements. Or you could try asking your friends for the URLs of their favourite sites – such as sites for bands, sites about films and TV shows, or sites about computer games. Your school might have a website. So might the place where your mum or dad works, or a club you belong to.

Have a guess

If you don't know the address of a site you want to look at, you can try guessing. Lots of bands, clubs and other organizations use the same name on the Web as they use in the real world. This means you can find them by typing:

www.

| www. |

then their name

| www.bigfishonline |

then either '.com', or '.co.uk' (if they're British). If that doesn't work, you could also try '.net' or '.org'.

| www.bigfishonline.co.uk |

Find your way back

Remember Hansel and Gretel dropping crumbs in the forest so they could get back home? Well, the crumbs got eaten by birds, but your browser's got a better way. You'll see 'Back' and 'Forward' buttons on your browser screen. If you lose your way while you're surfing, you can go back, a page at a time, until you find the page you want again. And if you want to go right back to your browser's starting screen in one jump, click on the 'Home' button.

Where's the map?

If you know where you want to go, but not how to get there, you need a search engine. A search engine does all the hard work of looking at lots of web pages for you, and finds the ones you might be interested in looking at.

How does it work?

A search engine uses a program called a spider to find out what's on the Web. The spider spends all its time crawling through all the web pages in the world, following links from one to the next. It makes a huge list of what subjects are on each web page. Then, when you ask the search engine for a particular subject, it can tell you quickly which are the best pages to try. There are lots of search engines to choose from, like AltaVista, Google, Mamma and Alltheweb. We haven't got space to give you a guide to them all, but they're mostly pretty similar and look a bit like this:

How do I use it?

You just type in a few words, called keywords, about the thing you want to find out about – such as:

recipe for popcorn

or:

world's tallest buildings

then hit the 'Search' button or the 'Return' or 'Enter' key on your keyboard. The search engine will show you links to lots of web pages. Chose one, click on it, and you're there!

Search

Welcome to FABSEARCH

Search the Web for:

[   ]   **Search**

Sport | News | Science
Travel | Jobs | Weather | Entertainment

Make your own map

When you find yourself at a really brilliant site, you'll want to make a note of where it is so you can go back another day. Luckily, you don't need to write down all the gobbledegook of the URL – that would take ages. Instead, your browser has a way of remembering your favourite sites for you. When you're at a page you really like, just click on the 'Bookmarks' or 'Favorites' button on your browser screen. The browser will then let you add that page to your own list of the sites you like best. Then, the next time you want to go there, you just click on 'Bookmarks' or 'Favorites' again, choose the site you want, and the browser will take you there at once. It's like having your own personal transporter!

Quicklinks
The **Internet @ction** website has links to several good search engines and directories that can help you find things quickly and easily. Try a few and see which one is your favourite.

On a plate

You don't always have to enter keywords to start searching. Instead, you could follow some of the links the search engine has already set up. All the big search engines have lists of categories like Sport, Entertainment, Travel, and so on. These go to more lists to narrow down your choice. Finally, you get to sets of pages the search engine has helpfully collected and sorted for you, all ready to go. Once you're there, you can wander around, following links to wherever you like.

Off the beaten track

If you wander through the categories suggested by a search engine, you should get to the sort of page you want and not stray into murky areas. But more and more pages show advertising now, and some of the adverts are for adult products that are not very nice. And sadly, there are quite a few dark corners on the Internet that can be upsetting – you might be frightened by what you see there. If you get somewhere you don't want to be, remember to use the 'Back' button to get out again quickly.

> You can even organize your list of bookmarks into sections to make them easier to find.

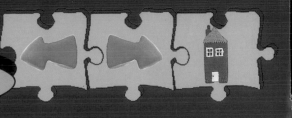

A search engine is good for – wait for it – searching! But you need to be smart to get the most from it. Here are some ways to make your searches extra clever and cunning, so you'll find what you want really quickly.

Searching high and low

There are millions of web pages out there – so there's a lot to look through. If you want to find out about cats, and you just type in:

cat

you'll be swamped! You'll suddenly find there are cats everywhere! There are thousands of pages that mention cats, and it would take you years to read them all. Instead, you need a way to make your search narrower. Well, it can be done.

Weird words

Very occasionally, you might get away with a single word search. For example, if you want to find out stuff about the Aztec god Quetzalcoatl, there may not be too many sites to look through because it's such an unusual word. But what if you find there's a car called a Quetzalcoatl? That's when things get tricky…

More or less

But not too tricky! You can narrow down your search to cut out all the car sites simply by adding a minus sign (-) before the word car. So you search for:

quetzalcoatl -car

If there are still too many sites, try:

quetzalcoatl -car +aztec

for sites that mention both Quetzalcoatl and the Aztecs. That should get rid of sites about cars, chocolate bars, rock stars and anything else you don't want!

Geek speak

You can use 'and' instead of + and 'not' instead of -, like this:

quetzalcoatl not car and aztec

If you want to be extra geeky, you can call this method 'Boolean searching'.

Find a phrase

Sometimes you want to look for words that are so common you don't stand much chance of finding what you want. For example, say you want to find out about black holes, so you type in:

> black +hole

You'll still get all the pages that contain the words 'black' and 'hole'. And that will include all sorts of stuff.

The common mole has soft, **black** fur and lives in a **hole** in the ground.

To solve this problem, put your keywords in quotation marks, to show the search engine that you're looking for a specific phrase, not just a few random words:

> "black hole"

You can even use use +, - and " " together, like this:

> "milky way" +galaxy -chocolate

Getting it right

The more exact you can be, the quicker you'll find what you want as you won't have to look through lots of irrelevant stuff. But if you're too fussy, there may be no pages with all the words you ask for, even if there are pages on the right topic. After a bit of practice, you'll get it right.

Only cool stuff, please

You can be quite picky when you use a search engine. Some will let you ask for sites in a particular language, or only pages that have pictures or sounds. This can be very useful, for example if you're looking for a photo or a piece of music. And remember, if something nasty crops up in your searches, you don't have to look at it. Just as your TV has an off button, your computer has a 'Back' button to help you get away fast.

Move home!

You don't need to stick with the home page set by your browser. You can move home as many times as you like on the Web, and you don't even need to pack. If you find a page you like, you can make it your home page – look through the tools and menus of your browser to find out how. Then your new home page will pop up as soon as you go on-line.

Don't be a couch potato!

Using a mouse isn't the best exercise in the world. And surfing the Web shouldn't mean that you're glued to the screen all day, vegging out. Remember, you can use the Internet to help you find cool things to do in the real world, too.

What do you like to do?

What do you do when you're not in front of the screen? Do you go rollerblading or swimming, go to Brownies, look after your pets, save the planet or hang out at the café? Fine – but how many times have you got to the pool and found it's closed, or found the price has gone up at the roller rink? The Web's not just a way to spend time when you've got nothing else to do. It can save you hassle in the real world too.

Find out from home

You should be pretty good at searching for things by now. So why not get together a list of useful local web addresses? It could include URLs of local places you like to go to so that you can check out what's going on before you step out of the door. Look up the URL of your local sports centre, cinema, football stadium, roller rink or ice rink... or anywhere you like to go.

Try this

- Can you find the opening hours, the charges, and listings of special events?

- See if there's a mailing list you can join. You'll be sent e-mails about events in advance, so you can get tickets before they sell out.

- You might even be able to book tickets or order brochures on-line.

Urgent – info needed!

The Web's a great place to find out things you need to know in a hurry. If you find an injured animal in your garden, there will be a site telling you how to look after it, or where to take it to. If you want to build a nest box for bats, change a tyre on your bike, or learn Braille or semaphore, the info's all there. It's just waiting to be found, using any search engine (see pages 12–15).

Quicklinks
To find a link to the Seti screensaver web page, click on Tools on the **Internet @ction** website.

Track an alien

Your computer can even keep working while you're off doing something more interesting. Get yourself a copy of the Seti screensaver (there's a link to the right page on our website) and your computer can take part in a global effort to process data collected from space over the last twenty years. You get a screensaver that displays colourful graphs. They're usually just random – but if there's a regular pattern, it could show a message from outer space. Who knows, you could be the first person to discover alien life forms!

Be useful

There are now so many people on the Internet that it's becoming a useful resource for researchers. You can do your bit to help the progress of science by taking part in a real experiment. You might need to count birds in your garden, or record the temperature every day for a week. Then you send in your data by e-mail, or fill in a form on a website. The work you've done is used by scientists carrying out real research. And they couldn't do it without you!

Thanks for all the help!

Local activities

The Web could also tell you about a sponsored charity event to take part in, a scheme to clean up a local pond, or where to recycle plastic drinks bottles. The best sites for this kind of thing are small websites run by local people. To find them, search for the name of your town or village on the Web.

Make an Internet snack

If you're planning a long browsing session, why not find a snack recipe first and then you can scoff while you surf? There are loads of recipes to be found on the Web for stuff yummy and disgusting from around the world!

OK, do be a couch potato!

Sometimes, all you want to do is veg out. Yes? Well, the Web is here to help. You can veg out totally, or (if you want to be really useful), you can help other people veg out!

Channel surfing

Anything on TV? Check on the Web! You can use your computer to find out what's on TV, and maybe even watch it. To watch real Web TV – proper broadcasts from terrestrial channels like BBC and Channel 4, or special web channels – you need a TV adaptor card for your computer. Ask a grown-up to buy and fit one if you want to do this. But there's not much point – you just end up paying to be on-line to watch stuff you can see on the real TV for free.

Go back in time

Why not have a retro day and watch TV from before you were born? Look for sound and video clips from long ago – maybe you could watch the first moon landing, listen to Elvis or see bits of TV series even your mum and dad are too young to remember.

You can set some search engines to look only for sites that have sound or video on them.

Surf to the stars

It's much more fun to look at sites about TV shows you already watch, and find out more about them. On some TV sites, you can send in your comments and questions or even chat to the stars. And if you've missed an episode, you can find out about what's happening in all the soaps and series.

What's on?

You can use the Web to help you find books to read and films to watch. There are reviews you can read to check out what other kids think of things. And if you're feeling energetic enough to move your fingers a bit, you can send in your own reviews of books you've read and movies you've seen, to help other people veg out with ease.

- Add to shopping cart
- Read reviews of this book
- I have read this book and would like to review it

The Haunting of Samphire Creek

This book is brilliant. I was so scared when I read it that I didn't even dare get out of bed to go to school! But it all turns out OK in the end.

By Heather McAllister, aged 9

The big on-line bookshops let you write reviews of your favourite books for everyone else in the world to read.

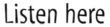

Listen here

Do you ever listen to the radio while you use the computer? Well, you can use your computer as a radio, too. There are loads of radio stations that don't broadcast over the airwaves at all – they just use the Web. You don't need to look at the web page while you listen, so you can do other things at the same time.

Quicklinks
We've provided links to some great vegging-out sites – including TV sites, book and film sites, and web radio stations. Just go to www.internetaction.co.uk.

Remember someone's probably paying for your on-line time. You might not be too popular if you stay tuned to a web radio station all day!

The Internet can take you to places you can't get to on your own – whether it's to a pop concert in New York or to outer space. How? By seeing the world through webcams!

What is a webcam?

A webcam is just what it sounds like – a camera linked to a computer on the Internet. Usually, a webcam takes a picture every few seconds or minutes and sends it out onto the Web, but some webcams broadcast live video.

Where can you go?

There are webcams all over the world and a few outside it, too! You can see some really exciting things, like solar and lunar eclipses, or polar bears in Canada – and some really boring things, like someone's toaster or floorboards. Here are just a few of the exciting web-watching opportunities waiting for you...

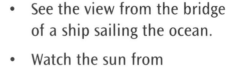

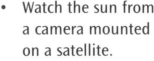

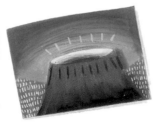

- See the view from the bridge of a ship sailing the ocean.
- Watch the sun from a camera mounted on a satellite.
- Stare at the tank of someone's pet chameleon.
- Visit an archaeological dig.
- Peer into the crater of an active volcano.
- Wait for ghosts to appear at a haunted spot.
- Go inside the Disney studios.
- Snoop around the kitchen of a pizza parlour.

You can even send postcards to friends from places you haven't been to. But watch out for spoofs: you don't want to be stuck looking at a wall for too long...

You can do that off-line!

Be there or be square

Loads of events are 'webcast' – which means broadcast over the Web. So if you can't get tickets for a special concert – or can't fly to Rio for the Carnival – you can still watch. You can be at all the cool gigs around the world without leaving your seat. Remember time zones, though – if a concert in New York is starting at 7pm, you might be in bed then – it's midnight in the UK!

History spot

The first ever webcam was set up by students at the University of Cambridge so that they could see if there was any coffee left in the coffee pot without going downstairs! You can still check their coffee pot, from anywhere in the world – and even listen to it.

Your own webcam

You can even get a web camera of your own and set up your own mini webcam at home. Quickcam is one type – it's a small, black-and-white camera that looks like a metal eyeball. You can plug it into your computer and send pics of yourself to your friends while you chat to them. Or you could point the camera at something else, like your goldfish tank or the view from your window.

Where to look

It's easy to travel the world by webcam, but unless you know where you're going, you'll need to stop off first at a webcam ring – a website that's got links to lots of active webcams.

> Some webcam rings award prizes for the best webcams.

Or just use a search engine (see pages 12–15). For example, to find sites that refer to webcams in Gdansk, type:

```
webcam +gdansk
```

Tell the search engine you want sites with a picture to miss out the pages that just refer to webcams. It's worth knowing where the webcams are in your local area – maybe your mum can check a webcam to see if you've skived off to the café instead of going to football!

Quicklinks
We've chosen some good webcam rings that will help you get started in the world of webcam viewing. Just go to the **Internet @ction** website for some great views.

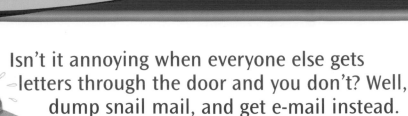

You've got mail!

Isn't it annoying when everyone else gets letters through the door and you don't? Well, dump snail mail, and get e-mail instead. That way you'll get the most post!

What's e-mail again?

E-mail is a way of sending messages around the world using the Internet. And even if you send it from the North Pole to the South Pole it costs only a few pence, and takes just seconds to get there!

How to do it

You usually get an e-mail account when you join an ISP or Internet Service Provider (see page 6), and you may have one up and running already. It's best to have your own private e-mail account and address, so no-one can snoop through your mail. This should be easy, now there are so many free ISPs. There are also some websites, such as Hotmail, that will give you a free e-mail address and let you send and receive messages.

Quicklinks
You'll find some links to sites that can provide you with an e-mail account on the **Internet @ction** website. See which one suits you.

What's your name?

When you start an e-mail account, you'll need to choose a name for yourself. It will look a bit like this:

This symbol stands for 'at'. It appears in the middle of all e-mail addresses.

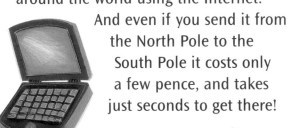

your_name@your_isp.com

This bit of the e-mail address shows who you are.

This is the name of your e-mail provider.

Remember that you can't have the same address as anyone else, or the e-mails would get mixed up. And all the common names are bound to have been taken already by other people. So don't just try 'kevin_jones@' or 'sarah_smith@'. You'll need to be a bit more imaginative – include your middle name, or make up a nickname. If your name's a bit unusual, though, you might be the first to try it – so give it a go:

sabina_stachiewicz@netcompany.com

Open sesame!

You'll probably need a password to collect your e-mail. This should be something no-one else can guess but that you can definitely remember! You can often set a hint question – then if you forget your password, you just answer the question correctly and the computer program tells you the password. But look out – if someone else can answer the question, they can find out your password, so you have to be a bit smart.

Get mailing

Once you've got an e-mail address, you can send mail to anyone else whose e-mail address you know – and some you don't. Lots of websites have a 'Mailto:' button or link – you just click on it to send e-mail to the owner of the page. You can get in touch with everyone from pop stars to politicians this way.

> You don't need to be on-line to write your e-mail. You just go on-line for a few seconds to send it.

When you want to send a new message to someone, here's what to do:

- Start a new message (click on 'New mail' or 'Compose').
- Type the e-mail address of the person you're sending it to.
- Add a few words about what's in the e-mail in the 'Subject' or 'About' line.
- Type your message.
- Send it! (click on 'Send now', or 'Send later' to send it next time you go on-line).

To:	sabina_stachiewicz@netcompany.com
Subject:	You're on the Net!

Hey Sab! Congratulations on getting on-line at last. I hope you're wearing those nice slippers I knitted you.

Lots of love,
Granny.

Send **New** **Reply** **Forward** **Delete**

E-mail is carried over the phone network – like everything you do on the Internet – so it gets where it's going almost immediately (as long as you're logged on). It's a great way to keep in touch with friends and grannies on the far side of the world. You don't have any friends on the far side of the world? Then it's time to get some! Find out how on the next page.

More mailing

Now that you're all set up to e-mail your friends and relatives, it's time to find out how to make new e-mail friendships and become a real whizz at the keyboard.

Need a friend?

It's easy to find an e-mail penpal. It could be someone from a different country or someone from just round the corner (get your friends to set up e-mail accounts, too). There are lots of websites to help you find penpals to e-mail. You can even set up a class e-mail exchange, so your class at school can link up with kids in Africa or Russia, or anywhere else you like.

> Things you send along with your e-mail are usually called 'attachments' or 'enclosures'.

Not just text

Once you've got used to sending text messages, you can be more adventurous and send extra stuff along with your message. Look in your e-mail software, or the website you send e-mail from, for info on how to attach files to e-mails (there's usually an 'Attach' button).

What can I send?

You can attach pictures, extra text, sounds or even animations to an e-mail. The main thing to remember is to make sure the files aren't too big, or they'll take too long to send and may get jumbled up. It's a bit like writing to a friend and sticking a picture in too – too much stuff will burst the envelope!

Addresses on a plate

You wouldn't try to remember all the postal addresses of everyone you ever wrote to, and you shouldn't expect to remember a whole load of e-mail addresses either. Luckily, you don't have to – all e-mail systems keep an address book to list the names and addresses of people you write to and get e-mail from. You can then just pick the person you want from the list and you don't even need to type their address – it will appear in the right place.

Writing back

When you get a mail you want to answer straight away, you just use the 'Reply' button to start a new message to the person who sent it. The message they sent is usually copied into your new message. You can add your text to it at the right places to answer their questions, or delete all or some of what they wrote.

Lots of friends?

Sometimes, you'll want to send a message to more than one person – maybe you're sending out party invitations, or even an e-zine (see pages 38-39 to find out about e-zines). To send a message out to lots of people at once, just put more than one name in the address space. You can also add lots of other addresses using the 'CC' (copy to) button or the 'Recipients' button.

Show your feelings!

When you're writing an e-mail message, it can be hard to get the right 'tone of voice' for your message. You can't use your voice or your handwriting to laugh out loud or emphasize something. But you can use smileys – also called emoticons. They're little sideways faces that you make using letters and symbols from the keyboard. They can show if you're sad, happy, joking or laughing. Try these...

:o)	happy
:-(	sad
:-O	surprised
:-D	laughing
<:-(	dunce
:o#)	moustache

... and then make up some of your own!

All e-mail programs are different, but they're usually easy to work out.

Quicklinks

We've put some links to penpal sites on the **Internet @ction** website. You may be able to find some more by searching with directories.

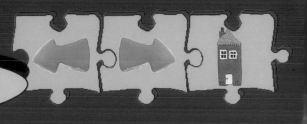

How many computer games have you got? Well, the Web's got more! You can check out all the different types of games and find your favourites, play test versions of new games, battle against other players on-line, and pick up handy game-playing tips.

Computer games

It's no surprise that you can play computer games on a computer. But the Web is a useful way to find out about new games, and even try them out, before you spend your pocket money or birthday booty.

Try these

Search for multi-level games, fantasy games, space-invaders-type games, flight or driving simulations – or anything you like! Play them on-line, or download samples to try out. The try-out is usually limited in some way, so you can't use it forever instead of buying the full game – you might get only one level, or the game might stop working after 30 days.

But it's better than nothing!

Web opponents

If you've bought a computer game, like Worms or Football, you might be able to find someone else on the Net to play against on-line. Look in the instruction book – it will tell you the URLs of websites to go to.

Not computer games

Computer games aren't the only games you can play on-line. There are computer versions of nearly any game you can think of – chess, Cluedo, Monopoly, Scrabble, hangman, and lots more. There are some games you can play on your own:

Matching pairs

Tetris

Sliding puzzles

Crosswords

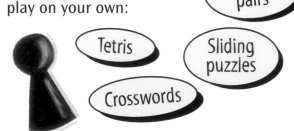

You can play other games against a friend, a stranger, or a computer:

Monopoly

Chess

Scrabble

Retro chic

The first ever computer game was called Pong – and you can play a version of the original Pong on the Web. You can also find lots of emulations (copies for modern computers) of games written for the funny old computers your dad might've used in the 80s.

Time zone trouble

If you want to play on-line games with kids in other countries, you might get a bit tangled up in all the different time zones. There's a cool way round this: work in Internet time! Internet time was invented by the Swiss watchmakers, Swatch. It's a way of marking time all over the world so that it's not affected by time zones.

Game gift

Make a great present by downloading copies of all the games your parents used to play and making them a special gift pack. You might even enjoy the games yourself!

How does it work?

Instead of boring old hours and minutes, Internet time divides the day into 1000 'beats'. The time is 000 at midnight in Basle (Swatch's hometown in Switzerland), 500 at midday in Basle, and so on. But instead of changing around the world, it's 000 or 500 everywhere. So you can arrange to meet on-line at 750 and it will be 750 for your friend in New Zealand or Namibia, Toronto or Timbuctu.

Quicklinks
The **Internet @ction** website has links to games sites galore. To go to them key in the website address www. internetaction.co.uk.

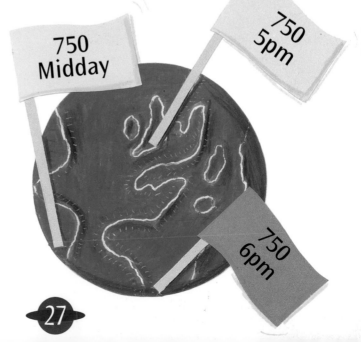

750
Midday

750
5pm

750
6pm

Ever forgotten to send a birthday card? You get extra time if you send a web card instead, as it gets there immediately. You don't even need a stamp!

Drop a line

There are loads of sites that let you send greetings to your friends. You can send birthday cards, cards for special festivals like Christmas, Divali or Hannukah – or just send a 'hello' or a postcard. And a web greetings card is often better than an ordinary one – it can have moving pictures and even sounds.

How do I do it?

It works like this. Once you've found the right website, you choose a picture – still or moving – and maybe a sound clip, too. Then you type a message and send your card to an e-mail address. Easy! Your friend gets an e-mail saying they have a card to pick up and showing the URL to go to. They have about ten days to look at it before it's removed to make room for someone else's card. And there's usually a 'Reply' button, so they might send a card back to you.

Wish you were here

If you just want to say hi, you can send a postcard instead. Lots of places let you send a postcard – from a faraway country, a zoo or theme park you've never been to, or a holiday resort you're not at!

Greetings from Timbuktu

Christmas card

If your friends aren't on-line, send a card to someone with a professional interest in getting letters from kids – like Santa. There are places that will forward your messages, and you may get a reply (but only if you're good!).

How does this thing work?

Sneaky tip
If you're really late, just change the date on your computer's clock and send an e-mail. The e-mail message will have that date on it and your friend (or granny) will just think it got delayed!

Quicklinks
At the **Internet @ction** website, we've selected some of the best card sites, some collections of clip art, and a few sites about the Romans and the parties they had.

Don't stop at cards

If it's Christmas or a birthday or some other occasion, you can get more than a card from the Web. There are loads of free pictures and symbols (called clip art) that you can use to make invitations, posters, place cards, mats, party bags – everything you need for your celebration.

Don't forget to look up your party recipes on the Web too!

Roman revels

So – pick a festival, or even make up an occasion, and have a party. Studying the Romans at school? Throw a Roman party!

■ Do invitations in Latin with Roman mosaic pictures.

■ Find some real Roman recipes for the meal (yuk – no wonder they made themselves sick!).

■ Cut out a load of coloured squares and get people to make up their own mosaics. For inspiration, you could print out some pictures of real Roman mosaics from the Web.

■ Check out a site on the Romans for some tips on how to tie your toga.

See how much stuff you can get from the Web to carry through your party theme. Don't forget to send the invites as web cards – and ask for a reply in the same way.

Please come to our
ROMAN
CONVIVIUM
(party)

Ch@tterbox

Do you get into trouble for nattering to your friends on the phone all the time? If you chat on-line instead, your mum can't hear what you say – and you can talk to more than one friend at once.

Chat? What's that?

On-line chat is a way of meeting up in cyberspace and 'talking' to other people. Except you don't really talk. You type what you want to say and it appears on their computer as soon as you've typed it. It's quicker than e-mail because you don't need to wait for the other person to pick up their message, so you can have a proper conversation. You can chat with your regular friends, or with friends you've met on-line.

In the chat room

Chat takes place in a chat room – a virtual space which you share with the people you're chatting to.

What's a virtual space?

It's an imaginary space created by computers.

Theme rooms

There are lots of chat rooms for kids, and they often have themes. Theme rooms help you find other people who want to talk about hockey or horses or football.

Find a chat room

If you want to chat with new people, just check into one of the free public chat rooms. Many Internet Service Providers organize chat rooms, and you can find them by searching on the Web. But first, you'll need to:

- Register with the chat service.
- Choose a nickname that people will know you by in the chat room.
- Choose a password. You'll need to remember it to get in.
- Choose a chat room to start in – look for the special kids' rooms.

Lurk and learn

Once you're in a chat room, it's best to watch quietly for a while to see how things go, and then launch in with your own comments. This way, you can see how it works and what everyone's talking about.

Quicklinks
Want to get chatting? Just go to the **Internet @ction** website and find our links to some good free chat services for kids.

Waiting quietly while other people chat is called lurking.

Chat to friends

If you want to chat with your schoolfriends, or with friends who live further away, fix up a time when you can all visit the same chat room. (You could use Internet time – see page 27.) You can even set up your own chat room, and hang out there knowing only your friends are going to turn up.

Fix a regular time to go to the chatroom, and you'll bump into them quite a bit. Check out your chat service to find out how to set up your own private room.

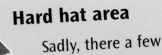

Hard hat area

Sadly, there a few weirdos who hang around chat rooms. You must never give out your real name, address or phone number in a chat room. And you should always use chat rooms that are intended for children and run by a responsible organization. These have moderators – people who watch what's going on to make sure nothing dangerous or frightening can happen to you. (But don't worry – they won't note what you say and tell your mum, dad or teachers!) If people misuse the chat room, they will be warned, or banned from coming back. It's a nice way of keeping the space safe for kids who just want to get together and gossip.

Get something for nothing

Ever bought a comic just to get the free gift on the front, or searched through the breakfast cereal to find the free plastic gimmick? Then free stuff on the Web is for you!

Please – have this!

Lots and lots of web pages are put up by people who've made something cool and want to share it. So there's loads of stuff out there, just waiting to be wanted. You can get clip art, jokes, games, screensavers, bits of video, sound clips, useful software – almost anything you need. You can even get an on-line pizza delivered to your screen while you work!

Quicklinks
The **Internet @ction** website has links to sites where you can get free cyberpets, screen savers, demos of games and much more.

Can't have a dog?

Why not have a cyberpet? It won't mess the carpet, doesn't eat too much and costs nothing. You don't need to clean it out or take it for a walk. And it doesn't even have to be a recognized species! You can get a boring old dog or cat, but why stop there? You could have a unicorn, a dinosaur, a dodo or a whole colony of space aliens. You can even get a virtual baby if you feel you need another brother or sister! Some cyberpets respond to what you do to them and develop or learn. But you can also get very simple ones that just sit there on your screen, look cute and wink at you. Just take your pick!

Finding free stuff

You can do a search for 'jokes' or 'clip art' – but you'll get a lot of hits. Try to be more specific and you'll get where you want to be faster:

> jokes +penguin

will get you jokes about penguins;

> "clip art" +Romans

will get you pics of Romans;

> cyberpet +dinosaur

might help you find the pet you want.

Ware to share

If you want software, the keyword to search for is 'shareware'. Shareware is software you can use for free. There is sometimes an honesty clause – if you want to carry on using it after you've tried it, you're supposed to pay for it, though it's usually not much.

You can also get lots of free demos of games and packages you might want to buy. You can try out one or two levels, or use it for a few weeks until it times out. This is long enough to find out whether you like it, and then you can pay for the full package if you do.

Small Print

Yawn – but you need to know it. Someone has put a lot of work into putting together all this clip art, making cartoon clips and writing free software. Play fair – check how you're allowed to use it and don't do anything else with it. Usually, you can put it in your own stuff, but not sell it to anyone else or publish it without permission. If everyone plays by the rules, people will carry on putting free stuff on the Web. But if we take advantage of it, more and more will be pay-to-use. It's also a bad idea to take things that are posted on the Web illegally, such as sound files stolen from albums, or bootleg releases of videos and films. These damage the film and music industries and cost people their jobs.

Windows™ shopping

Don't you just hate trailing around the shops with a grown-up? Shop on-line instead: you can go off on your own, you won't get tired, you can stop when you're bored, and it's more eco-friendly than driving into town.

Shop till you drop

Lots of the shops you go to in the real world are on-line, too. The Web's great for window-shopping – you can find books, videos, music and toys on-line. You can also check out the clothes shops to see what's around before you go out in the cold. Then make a detailed list, and your shopping trip will be quick and hassle-free. It's a good way of deciding what you want for your birthday or Christmas, too. Most of the big toy and game shops have websites. You can often try out games on-line, or download a sample to try before you buy. And you can listen to clips of music to help you decide if you want to buy that new album.

Wish-list

Committed shopaholics browse at leisure, then copy text and pictures out of the web pages into a new document and make themselves a detailed list. If you think someone will buy on-line for you, you can even make up a list with the URLs of the sites where you found the stuff, and they can just follow the links and buy. A few sites for kids' things even have a shopping list compiler, so you can build up your shopping list with all the links in place and just pass it on to the person with the dosh.

> I've found a few things on the Web that I'd like for my birthday...

> Just search for the names of your favourite shops.

SURF

Beenz bonanza

The trouble with money is you need to have some before you can spend it, and that means doing some work for someone or saving your pocket money. But the Web has a better answer.

When you're on-line, you can save and use a special currency, called beenz. You get paid beenz by visiting websites, taking part in surveys and other activities you'll be doing anyway. You can count your beenz, and hoard or spend them – just like pocket money! You can spend beenz on playing games on-line, or on listening to music on-line, and you can even get money-off vouchers to use for real web shopping. You can give your beenz to charities on-line, too.

E-cash

If you want real money to spend on your e-shopping sprees, ask someone to set up a pocket money e-cash account for you. Some of the big banks are starting these up so that wired kids can shop on-line. You get a friendly grown-up to pay, say, £5 a month into an e-cash wallet and then you can spend it on-line. (Only at approved sites, though – so no deliveries of beer and pizza). You can't go overdrawn or borrow on your account, so when you run out of cash you have to wait till your wallet is topped up – just like real pocket money.

Magic cow cyberpet
Only 6 beenz!

Look at your bank's website to see if they do e-cash.

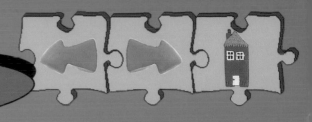

Ever fancied your chances as the next J. K. Rowling or Jacqueline Wilson? The Web could give you your big break – or at least a bit of practice and some ideas.

Get it together

A great thing about the Web is that you don't need to do all the work yourself – there are millions of people out there who want to join in too. So if you don't want to write a whole story, you can check into a story-building site. Lots of people add a little bit and the story builds up over time. This is great fun, as everyone's ideas are different and the stories can end up being really imaginative.

Write now!

If you write stories or poems, there are lots of websites that are ready to show off your work. Write up your story, save it as a plain text file (look in your word processor menus to find out how) and e-mail it to a site that publishes kids' writing. Check out the site first to make sure your story is the right type and the right length for them.

Can't type?

Don't let that stop you! There are sites which have a computer to write for you – you pick, say, the characters and some episodes, and the computer writes all the bits to join them together.

You might be able to put in a picture, too.

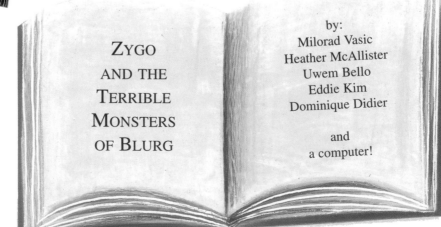

ZYGO AND THE TERRIBLE MONSTERS OF BLURG

by:
Milorad Vasic
Heather McAllister
Uwem Bello
Eddie Kim
Dominique Didier

and
a computer!

For your eyes only

You don't have to share your story-building with strangers. You could just set up a circle of friends to write stories by e-mail. One of you starts the ball rolling with the first paragraph, then e-mails it on to the next person. That person adds a paragraph and e-mails it on again – and so on.

Quicklinks
At the **Internet @ction** website you'll find links to sites where you can publish and broadcast your stories and art for all the world to see.

■ You'll need to agree a few ground rules before you start – like when each person's turn is, who's allowed to finish the story and how long each person's section can be.

In the picture

Why stop at stories? If you're getting together with friends, you can build up a picture together instead. Make sure you all have painting programs that can share one type of file – .gif files are good as they're small and easy to send by e-mail. Start off the picture and e-mail it on to the next person to add their bit.

■ You could pick a day in the school holidays, all sit down at your computers and knock off your masterpiece in a morning. Or you could spend weeks on it.

■ When you're writing with friends, you can write about people and places you all know. It makes it more special and personal.

■ Don't forget that even friends who've moved away can join in – if they've got e-mail.

You might get a basic painting program with your computer.

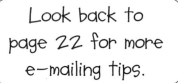

Look back to page 22 for more e-mailing tips.

(Mag)e-zines

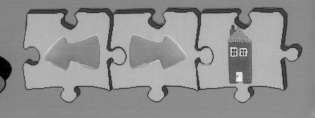

Get a magazine you can't line the bottom of your hamster cage with! Besides being ecologically sound and arriving at the speed of light, an e-zine can have bits a paper magazine can't – animated cartoons, sounds, and interactive games and quizzes.

A what?

An e-zine is an on-line magazine. Some are sent to your e-mail address for you to read – you subscribe to them by leaving your e-mail address at their website. Others sit on websites and wait for you to go and read them on-line.

Plug-in and play

For some e-zines, you might need special bits of software called plug-ins. A plug-in is a free program that allows your computer to play some special types of high-quality pictures or sounds. You might find you need tools like a Shockwave player, or something to display Quicktime movies. You can download plug-ins from the Web.

From the e-zine sites there are usually links to the plug-ins that you need.

Posh vs. free

You have to pay for the coolest e-zines (though they don't cost much). But there are also plenty of free e-zines which are just text, or text and a few pictures. Watch out, as some of them are just a way of pushing advertising at you – but you can still enjoy them!

Quicklinks
You'll find links to some great e-zines and e-zine sites on the **Internet @ction** website.

Take part

There are lots of e-zines out there on all sorts of subjects, and you're bound to find some you like.

Kidzine

Fab Fonts

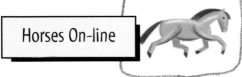

Horses On-line

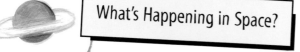

What's Happening in Space?

Computer Gamezine

Or make your own!

Have you got a secret club with your friends? Maybe you already pass notes around or have a magazine for your club. An e-zine is even better. If you want to make an e-zine to share with your friends, agree between you whether it will be just text that you e-mail or whether you want to do something more ambitious. If you all use the same word processor, you can make your e-zine with that and put in pictures, colours and fancy text, then e-mail it as an attachment (see page 24). You'll also have to collect the e-mail addresses of everyone who wants to subscribe. If it's a real success, read the next page to find out how to put it on a website and get other kids reading it!

After you've got used to what goes in the e-zines you read, why not contribute yourself? You'll find an e-mail address on the website or in the e-zine that tells you how to send in your own stories and pictures, reviews and games ideas. The Web only works so well because people are willing to do things for free and share what they know. So give something back and be part of the wired community.

Now you've surfed all over the Web, you'll know what makes a good site and what makes a bad site. Isn't it time you had a go at making your own website, and sharing your ideas with the world?

Plan ahead

You won't create a masterpiece of a website without a bit of planning. So before you start work at the computer, get a piece of paper and think through what you're going to do. Will the page be about you, or your pets or your home town? Or about something you're interested in, a club you belong to, or something you do with your friends? It makes it much easier if you decide first.

Make sure you save your pictures as .gif or .jpg files, with names no longer than eight letters.

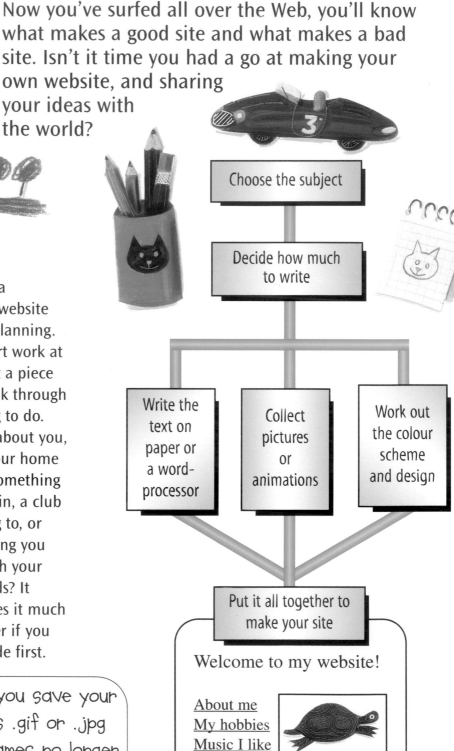

Choose the subject

Decide how much to write

Write the text on paper or a word-processor

Collect pictures or animations

Work out the colour scheme and design

Put it all together to make your site

Welcome to my website!

About me
My hobbies
Music I like
Links

My pet tortoise, Max

Getting it all together

Once you've worked out what you're doing, you'll need to write the text and collect or create the pictures. If you write your text in a word processor, make sure you save it as plain text (also called ASCII). There will be an option in your word processor's menus to do this. Don't use any special styling such as bold or italics – you'll be adding this when you turn it into a web page. You will probably want to put some pictures in your web page, too. There are lots of ways to get pictures:

- ■ You can draw them in a painting program on your computer.

- ■ You can draw them on paper and scan them in, if you have a scanner.

- ■ You can use clip art that you've got from a CD-ROM or found on the Web (check that you're allowed to use it in your own website).

- ■ You can take photos with a digital camera and load them into your computer. Or you can scan in normal photos.

Creating your page

When you've gathered together all your bits and pieces into a folder, you're ready to start making your page! You can use special web authoring software to help you create your web page. Or, if you don't have any, you can just use any text editor or word processor. Web authoring software gives you an easy way of putting together text and pictures and making links. You can see what your page will look like, and there will be easy ways of changing the colours and type styles. If you have a web authoring program, follow the instructions that come with it.

Don't panic!

But even if you don't have special software, you can still create web pages. The next couple of pages take you through putting together a simple web page using just a text editor. The next page also tells you how to put your page up on the Web when you've done it – so get to work!

Quicklinks
Follow the links from the **Internet @ction** website to find clip art to use in your web pages, and track down web authoring software you can get for free. Just go to www.internetaction.co.uk.

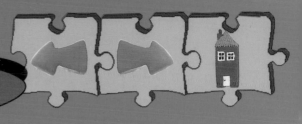

←-If you don't have any special software to help you create web pages, you can use any word processor or simple text editor, such as Notepad®.

HTML

Web pages are written in HTML – short for Hypertext Mark-Up Language. This uses special 'tags', written inside angle brackets, that tell the computer how to show text and pictures on a web page. The easiest way to get started is to do some web page authoring yourself. So follow the instructions to create a simple page. All you need to get started is this:

```
<html>
<head>
<title>My page</title>
</head>
<body>
Yo!
</body>
</html>
```

How it works

If you type what's in the yellow box into your text program, and save it with the name webpage.htm, you'll be able to open it using your web browser. It will look like this:

> Yo!

It's that simple!

These are the tags it uses. They are the minimum tags you need for a web page:

<html>
tells the browser that this is a web page.

<head> </head>
mark the start and end of the info the browser needs about the page. In our 'head' we just have the title of the page.

<title> </title>
go around the name of the web page – 'My page'. (This appears as the name of the window on the web page.)

<body> </body>
mark the start and end of the stuff that will actually be shown on the page (in this case, the word Yo!). All the text and pictures come between these two.

Finally, the </html> tag tells the browser it's got to the end of page.

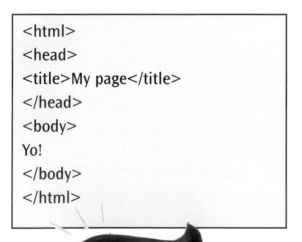

> Now it's time to do something cool...

All about Kevin

Here's a more advanced web page, about a funny monster called Kevin. It has a black background, some text about Kevin and a picture of him. Below, you can see what the HTML for this page looks like:

```
<html>
<head>
<title>Luki's page about Kevin</title>
</head>
<body bgcolor="black" text="white">
<p><font face="Arial"><strong>All
about Kevin</strong></font></p>
<p><font face="Arial">Kevin is a
monster. He lives in my wardrobe. He is
three years old.</font></p>
<p><font face="Arial">Kevin came out
of an egg. The egg had to be kept noisy
for three months before it hatched.
</font></p>
<p><font face="Arial">Kevin is green
and furry with purple spots. He has a
pom-pom tail that glows in the dark. He
only comes out at night. He eats black
dogs and pomegranates.
</font></p>
<p><font face="Arial">Here is a
picture of Kevin:</font></p>
<p align="center">
<img src="kevin.gif"></p>
</body>
</html>
```

If you copy this to make your own web page, you can try making these changes:

- Put your own title in place of 'Luki's page about Kevin' (shown in green).

- Change the background and text colours by writing other colours in the pink areas.

- Put your own text in the orange areas. New sections should start with <p> and end with </p>.

- Change the type style (shown in blue) by inserting another font such as "Verdana".

- Put another picture in the same folder as the web page and then put its name in the <img src> tag (shown in purple).

Post to a host

When you've finished, put your page on the Web! Your Internet Service Provider will probably provide free web space – just ask them how to upload your page. Remember to keep all the files you've used for your site grouped together, so that nothing is missing.

Here are a few extra pointers to help you get the most from the Internet.

Web browsers

You won't get the best out of the Web if you don't have a good browser. The browser is the software you use to surf the Web. You're most likely to have Internet Explorer or Netscape Navigator (or Communicator).

To check that you've got the most up-to-date version, check out Netscape's website for Navigator/Communicator or Microsoft's website for Internet Explorer. (You can find them easily by searching on the Web.)

There are other browsers, too. If you want to experiment, and it's your own computer, do a search for browsers. Remember you'll need to download the right version for your computer – a Windows browser won't work on a Mac and a Mac browser won't work on a PC.

Plug-ins

Sooner or later, you'll come across websites that only look their best if you have a 'plug-in' – an extra piece of software that improves your browser's performance. The plug-ins you're most likely to need are:

■ **Flash** Used for fast animations and good-quality line drawings that download quickly.

■ **Shockwave** For fast and whizzy interactive sites. Lots of games use Shockwave.

■ **.pdf files** For Adobe Acrobat Reader files. This is a way of putting printed pages on the Web. It lets you look at pages on screen just as they would appear if you printed them out. Some have spaces for you to type in, and they can have colour, sound and links, too.

Usually, a site that needs a plug-in will help you download the right one. You just click on the link to download and run the plug-in you need. Often, there is also an alternative version of the site you can use if you don't want the plug-in – for example, if you don't have much time or if you're using an old computer.

Want a cookie?

A cookie is a bit of software that's installed in your browser by some websites. It will remember the choices you've made and the things you've done when you've been visiting a particular site. The people who run the website can then use this info to see how surfers use the site.

Some computers are set up to accept cookies, and some are not. Sometimes you are given the option of taking a cookie. You should say yes if you don't mind letting the people who run the website see what your favourite parts of it are. For example, if they know you use their games but not their news pages, they might add more games.

The site will still work if you don't take the cookie – it just won't remember you!

If anyone else uses your computer, ask a grown-up to read this page and make settings that will keep your stuff separate from theirs. It will give you all some privacy. If no one else uses your computer, it's still worth asking a grown-up to install some software to keep you safe from being sent some of the more yukky stuff out there.

Grown-ups start here

If you use the computer yourself, there are probably things you use it for that you'd rather your children didn't interfere with. You might look at websites you don't want them to use. You might shop on-line or you might log into a work computer from home. Set up a user profile for each user so that their settings and preferences are kept for them alone

For Windows PC, do this:

1. Click the Start button on the toolbar. Choose Control Panel from the Settings submenu.

2. Choose Passwords. Go to the User profiles tab and turn on 'Users can customise their preferences…' and the user profile settings you want to be able to set. Close this box.

3. If you are using Windows 98, open Users from the Control Panel. This lets you create new users. It will take you through the stages of doing it. For maximum privacy, set all the options for personal settings that are offered. For more information, got to Help (from the Start menu).

4. If you are using Windows 95, restart the computer. It will ask for a log on name and password when it restarts. It will also ask whether you want to save settings for this user profile. You can repeat this as many times as you need to add more new users.

If you are using Mac, you should be able to set user profiles. To do this:

1. Choose Control panels from the Apple menu.

2. Choose Users and Groups and then choose New user. You can set a name and password for the new user. You can set as many users as needed.

Tell the other users the name and password you have set for them and how to use them. They can then set their own backgrounds, keep lists of their favourite websites, set their own home page and really make it their own space. The computer will keep their settings separate from everyone else's and use them whenever they log on.

Staying safe

To help keep your children safe on the Net:

- Insist they only go on-line when you're around.

- Set up the computer to need a password before it will connect to the Internet.

- Warn them about unpleasant content on the Internet and ask them to tell you if they see anything nasty or distressing.

- Check the **Internet @ction** website for links to software to filter web pages to check their content, and for other safety information.

USEFUL WORDS

You may come across some unfamiliar terms in this book or in the websites you visit. Here are a few useful explanations.

address book
A list of people's names and their e-mail addresses.

ASCII
Plain text, with no special styling or arrangement.

attachment
An extra file or document sent with an e-mail message.

Bookmark
See 'Favorites'.

Boolean search
A kind of advanced search that uses special instructions such as 'and' or 'not' (or + or -).

browse
To follow links around the Web to look at different pages.

browser
A program that can request web pages from a web server and display them on your computer screen. Also known as a web browser.

button
A clickable icon used on a web page or in a piece of software.

cc
Stands for 'copy to' in an e-mail program. You type a name in the 'cc' line to send a copy of your message to another person.

chat
A way of using the Internet to send messages between people who are on-line at the same time. What one person types can immediately be read by everyone else who is chatting.

clip art
Ready-made pictures you can collect from the Web to use in your own work.

cookie
A mini-program sent from a web page to live inside your browser. It saves your settings and choices relating to a particular website.

copyright or ©
A law that protects writers and artists from having their work copied without being paid.

cybercafé
A café with computers where people can use the Internet.

cyberpet
A virtual pet that lives in your computer.

cyberspace
The 'space' you travel around when surfing on the Net. In fact, cyberspace is simply made up of all the linked computers in the world.

database
An organized collection of information.

directory
A website that has an organized list of links to other websites.

download
To copy information from a computer on the Internet onto your own computer.

e-cash
A small amount of virtual money that you can only spend on-line.

e-mail (short for electronic mail)
A way of sending messages over the Internet to other Internet users.

e-mail address
The unique address people use to send you your e-mail.

emulation
A copy of a computer program that does the same as the original, but runs on a different computer.

enclosure
See 'attachment'.

e-zine
An electronic magazine published on the Web or delivered by e-mail.

FAQs
'Frequently Asked Questions' – a list of common questions and their answers, often found on websites.

Favorites
URLs that your browser knows you want to be able to visit easily. You can keep a list of Favorites and add to them when you find a site you like. Also known as Bookmarks.

gif
'Graphics Interchange Format' – a way of storing pictures on a computer. A lot of pictures on the Web have filenames ending in '.gif'.

hint question
A question that will help you to remember your password if you forget it. Always set hint questions that you know you will get right.

history
A record kept by your browser of all the websites you have visited.

hit
A request for a web page or part of a web page. Whenever a browser asks for a page from a server, it is a 'hit'.

home page
Either the first page your browser displays when you start it up, or the main page of a website.

host
An ISP or other service that will put your web page on their computer to make it available on the Web.

HTML
'Hypertext Mark-up Language'
– the computer language used
to write web pages.

http
Short for 'hypertext transfer
protocol' – rules that control how
information moves around the Net.

Hypertext Mark-up Language
See 'HTML'.

icon
A small picture on a computer
screen, usually used to represent
something.

Internet
A worldwide computer network.

Internet Service Provider (ISP)
An organization that connects
your computer to the Internet,
through their computers.

Internet time
A system of measuring time, based
on dividing the day into 1000 'beats'
and having the same time all over
the world. (500 is midday in
Switzerland, but 11am in the UK.)

ISP
See 'Internet Service Provider'.

jpeg
A format for graphics files. Jpeg
pictures have filenames ending
in '.jpg'.

keyword
A word you type into a search
engine to do a search.

link
A connection between two web
pages. On the Web, clicking on a
link will take you to another page.

mailto:
A button on a website. You click
on it to send an e-mail to the
people who own or run the site.

modem
A device that converts computer
data into sounds that can be sent
over ordinary telephone lines.

moderator
A person who checks chat rooms to
make sure people behave properly.

netiquette
The rules of good behaviour that
help everyone get along on the Net.

off-line
Not currently connected
to the Internet.

on-line
Connected to the Internet.

password
A word or phrase you sometimes
need to type in to get onto a
computer or read information.

plug-in
An extra bit of software your
browser can use to look at special
types of information.

ring
A group of websites on a similar
subject, all linked together.

scanner
A machine that can copy pictures
into your computer.

screensaver
A moving display that takes over
your screen when the computer
is turned on but not being used.

search engine
A website that stores information
about other web pages and lets
you search it for different subjects.

shareware
Software you can get for free. You
may be expected to pay a small fee
if you decide to keep it and use it.

snail mail
The ordinary postal service.

spam
Unwanted e-mail.

spider
A program that follows links
between web pages, and sends
information about the pages it finds
back to a search engine or directory.

surf
To wander around the Web, linking
from one page to another for fun.

tag
A code used in HTML to tell a
browser how to display a web page.

URL
'Uniform Resource Locator' – the
'address' of a page on the Web.

virtual
Something that exists in cyberspace
but has no physical existence.

web address
What you have to type to get
to a particular website.

web browser
A program that can request web
pages from a web server and display
them on screen. Web browsers are
often simply known as browsers.

webcam
A camera that feeds still or moving
pictures directly onto the Web.

webcast
A broadcast of a live event, such
as a concert, over the Web.

web page
A screen full of information,
including text, pictures and perhaps
sound and video, that is part of the
World Wide Web.

web radio
Radio stations that are broadcast
over the Web.

website
A collection of web pages put up by
one person or organization, usually
all about the same subject.

World Wide Web
A collection of information of all
types stored on computers all over
the Internet.

INDEX